curious about

BLACKTIP REEF SHARKS

BY EMMA ALICE JOHNSON

AMICUS LEARNING

What are you

curious about?

Curious About is published by
Amicus Learning, an imprint of Amicus
P.O. Box 227, Mankato, MN 56002
www.amicuspublishing.us

Editor: Ana Brauer
Series Designer: Kathleen Petelinsek
Book Designer and Photo Researcher: Sara Hood

Library of Congress Cataloging-in-Publication Data
Names: Johnson, Emma (Emma Alice), author.
Title: Curious about blacktip reef sharks / Emma Alice Johnson. Other titles: Blacktip reef sharks
Description: Mankato, MN : Amicus Learning, an imprint of Amicus, [2026] | Series: Curious about sharks | Includes bibliographical references and index. | Audience: Ages 6–9 | Audience: Grades 2–3 | Summary: "Do blacktip reef sharks hunt in packs? Learn about this intriguing ocean animal in a question-and-answer book for elementary-aged readers. Includes infographics, table of contents, glossary, books and websites for further research, and index"— Provided by publisher.
Identifiers: LCCN 2024048310 (print) | LCCN 2024048311 (ebook) | ISBN 9798892005029 (library binding) | ISBN 9798892005562 (paperback) | ISBN 9798892006101 (ebook)
Subjects: LCSH: Blacktip shark—Juvenile literature.
Classification: LCC QL638.95.C3 J638 2026 (print) | LCC QL638.95.C3 (ebook) | DDC 597.3/4—dc23/eng/20241226
LC record available at https://lccn.loc.gov/2024048310
LC ebook record available at https://lccn.loc.gov/2024048311

Photo Credits: Alamy Stock Photo/Arco / F. Schneider, 2, 14–15, Blue Planet Archive TRO, 2, 4, cbimages, 17, Reinhard Dirscherl, 20, WaterFrame_fba, 8; Dreamstime/Diego Grandi, 12, Isselee, cover, 1, Yann Hubert, 7; Getty Images/M Swiet Productions, 13, Torsten Velden, 3, 18–19, Westend61, 21; Shutterstock/Alessandro De Maddalena, 9 (middle), cbpix, 10–11, Fiona Ayerst, 9 (second from bottom), OHishiapply, 9 (top), Tetsuo Arada, 9 (second from top), Ton Wanniwat, 9 (bottom); The Noun Project/Hey Rabbit, 22, Patricia Lara, 22, Vectors Market, 23, Wahyuntitle, 23; Vecteezy/om1947, 16

Printed in India

CHAPTER ONE 1

Blacktip reef sharks have a lifespan of 10 to 12 years.

How big are blacktip reef sharks?

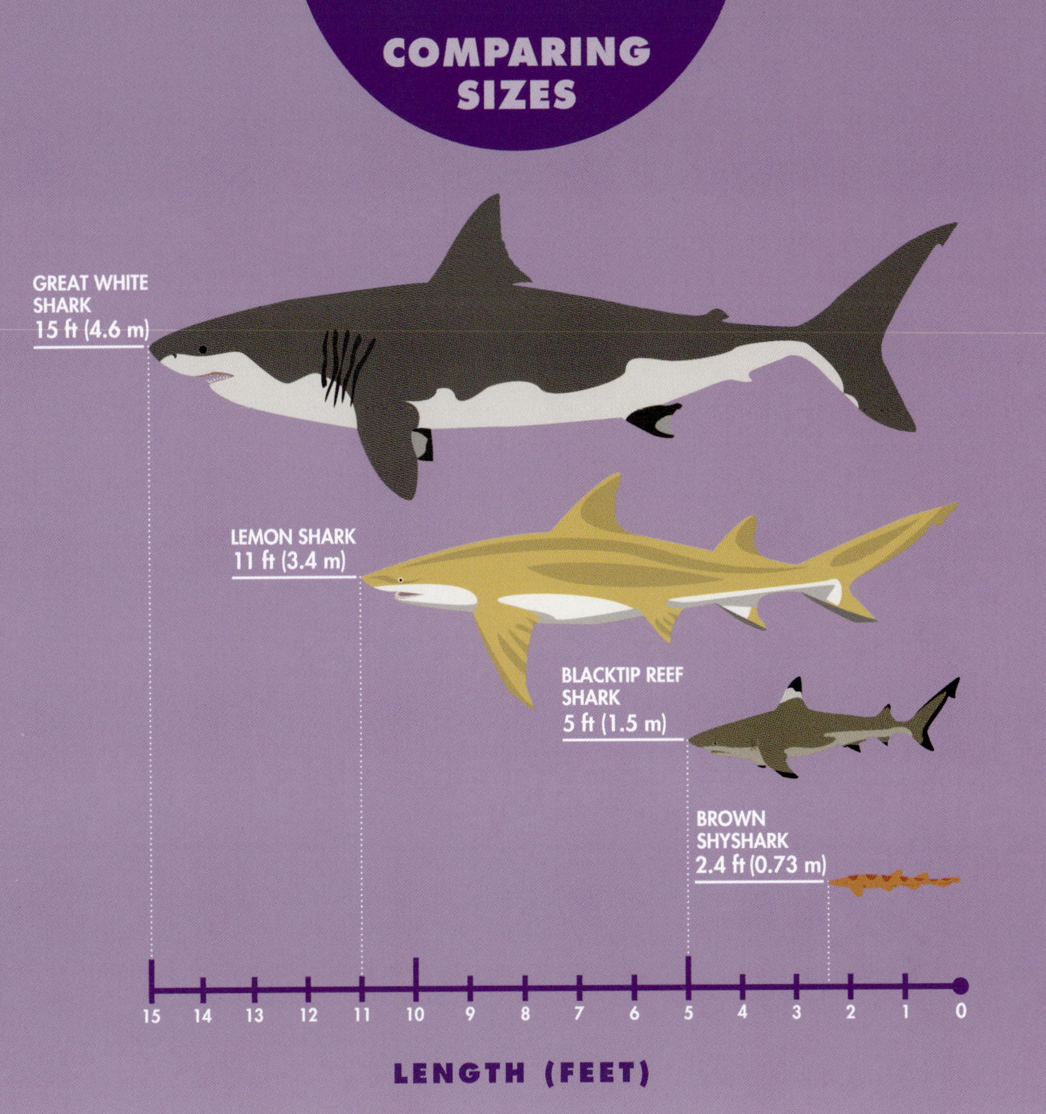

Blacktip **reef** sharks are medium-sized sharks. They are usually about 5 feet (1.5 meters) long. They may not be big, but they are fast **predators**. They can swim at speeds up to 20 miles (32.2 kilometers) per hour.

Why do their fins have black tips?

Scientists are not really sure! Blacktip reef sharks are gray on top and white on bottom. This coloring helps them hide. Their dark **fins** could be for identification. The sharks' black tips are all a little different. They are like your fingerprints!

The sharks' colors help them blend in with the ocean floor.

Do other sharks have black tips?

Blacktip reef sharks are often confused with blacktip sharks (pictured).

Yes. Blacktip sharks have fins with black tips too. They are in the same family as blacktip reef sharks. Blacktip sharks are bigger. They live in deeper water. Another similar shark is the whitetip reef shark. They have white tips on their fins!

BLACKTIP REEF SHARK

WHITETIP REEF SHARK

GREAT WHITE SHARK

TIGER SHARK

NURSE SHARK

CHAPTER TWO

How do blacktip reef sharks hunt?

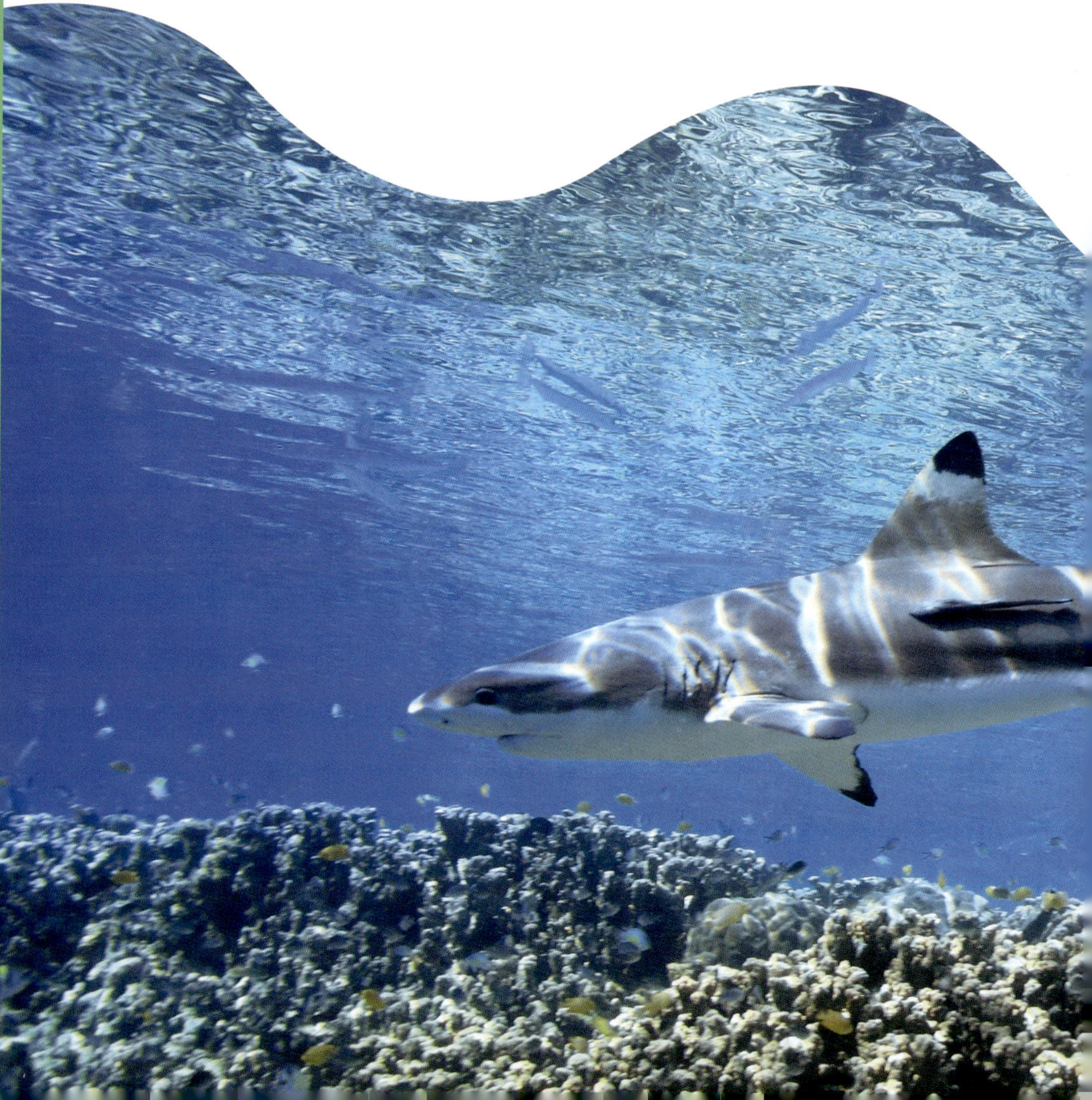

Most sharks hunt alone. But these sharks hunt in small groups. The group is led by the biggest shark. They work together to catch their **prey**. They will hunt an entire school of fish. That way each shark gets enough food.

Blacktip reef sharks hunt in warm, shallow waters.

What do blacktip reef sharks hunt?

They hunt small, brightly colored fish. Sharks do not see colors well. Bright fish are easy to see in dark reefs. They eat reef fish such as surgeonfish. The sharks also eat snakes or baby turtles when they are really hungry!

Hunting in groups keeps the sharks safe from bigger predators.

Can I see a blacktip reef shark hunting?

Yes. The sharks hunt in shallow water. They stick their **dorsal** fin out of the water when they swim. Sometimes they jump out of the water when they are hunting. They get excited about food!

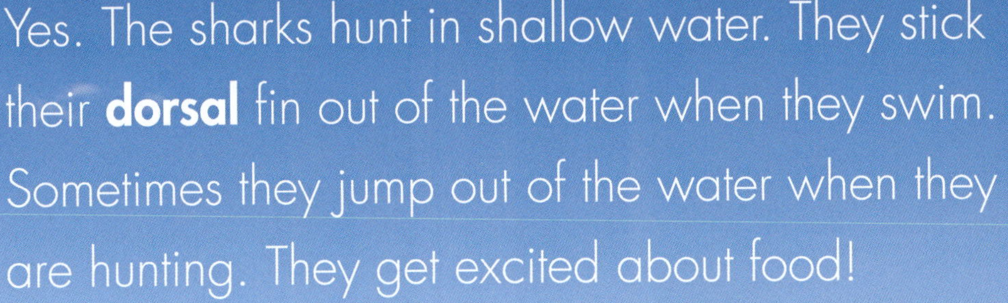

Lots of fish live around **coral** reefs. This is where the sharks hunt.

CHAPTER THREE

Where do blacktip reef sharks live?

They live in coral reefs. Most live in the Pacific Ocean and the Indian Ocean. Many blacktip reef sharks are found near Australia. They like to be close to shore. They do not like deep water. It gives their prey too much room to swim away!

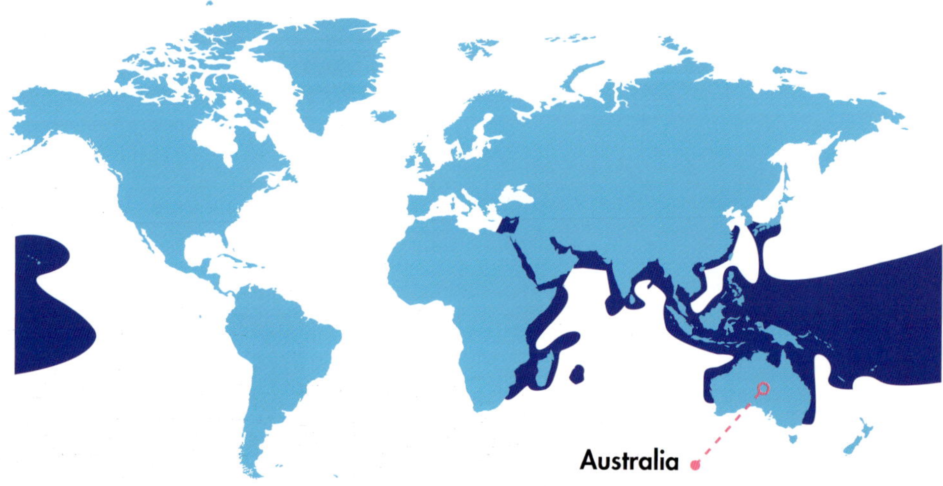

You may spot a blacktip reef shark when swimming around a coral reef.

Do blacktip reef sharks travel far?

Scientists can track how far sharks travel by using tags.

No. Blacktip reef sharks are homebodies. They live in the same place for years. Their home range is less than 1 mile (1.6 km). Some female sharks go farther to have babies. But they almost always return to their home range.

Are blacktip reef sharks endangered?

No. They are safe for now. But they might not be in the future. Their coral reef homes are dying. This is because of pollution and climate change. When the reefs die, the animals that live in them will also die or leave. If we protect the reefs, we can also protect these sharks!

DID YOU KNOW?
Coral reefs are home to 25 percent of all ocean life.

Overfishing of the sharks' prey also puts them at risk.

ASK MORE QUESTIONS

How many babies do blacktip reef sharks have at a time?

Where is the best place to see blacktip reef sharks?

Try a BIG QUESTION: What is being done to protect coral reefs?

SEARCH FOR ANSWERS

Search the library catalog or the Internet.
A librarian, teacher, or parent can help you.

Using Keywords
Find the looking glass.

Keywords are the most important words in your question.

If you want to know about:

- blacktip reef shark babies, type: BLACKTIP REEF SHARK PUPS
- where to find blacktip reef sharks, type: BLACKTIP REEF SHARK LOCATIONS

FIND GOOD SOURCES

Here are some good, safe sources you can use in your research.
Your librarian can help you find more.

Books

Blacktip Reef Sharks
by Julie Murray, 2020.

The World of Coral Reefs
by Erin Spencer and Alexandria Neonakis, 2022.

Internet Sites

National Aquarium | Blacktip Reef Sharks
https://aqua.org/explore/animals/blacktip-reef-shark
National Aquarium has an entire exhibit of blacktip reef sharks.

Ocean Conservancy | Blacktip Reef Sharks
https://oceanconservancy.org/wildlife-factsheet/blacktip-reef-shark/
Ocean Conservancy works to protect sharks and other ocean life from overfishing and other threats.

SHARE AND TAKE ACTION

Read a book about coral reefs.
What other animals live with blacktip reef sharks?

Imagine what a shark fin looks like when it pops out of the water.
Draw and color a blacktip reef shark dorsal fin.

With an adult, visit an aquarium.
See if you can find blacktip reef sharks or other reef life.

GLOSSARY

coral A small animal that lives on rocks underwater.

dorsal The back or top side of an animal.

fin A triangular body part on fish that helps them swim.

predator An animal that hunts other animals for food.

prey An animal hunted or killed for food.

reef A ridge of rocks or sand near the surface of the ocean.

INDEX

About the Author

Emma Alice Johnson lives on a farm in the woods. She grows flowers and loves insects. Bumblebees are her favorite insects. She is friends with a cat, a pig, and a bunch of chickens. She once swam with nurse sharks!